ZOO of DREAMS

poems by **ADRIAN MITCHELL**
and **Daisy**

pictures by **PETER BAILEY**

ORCHARD BOOKS

To the many Dog friends I meet on my daily walks.
They include Amra, April, little Archie, Avril, Barney,
Becky, Boris, Charlie, Chrissie, two other Daisies, Dylan,
the extremely handsome George, Millie, Mr Toby,
Pepper, Ping, Sam, Tosca, Tramp and Trouble.
And to my cats – Billie and Gnasher.
Also to my Aunts – Pippa, Polly and Ella
and to my very first human friends,
Mr and Mrs Chalkley of Pondcroft Barn.
Love
Daisy the Dog of Peace

For Siân, Owain and Anwen
P B

ZOO of DREAMS

ORCHARD BOOKS
96 Leonard Street, London EC2A 4XD
Orchard Books Australia
Unit 31/56 O'Riordan Street, Alexandria, NSW 2015
First published in Great Britain in 2001
ISBN 1 84121 817 0
A CIP catalogue record for this book
is available from the British Library
10 9 8 7 6 5 4 3 2 1
Printed in Great Britain

Contents

A Letter From the Poet

Dear Reader,

My full name is Daisy the Dog of Peace. I am a beautiful Golden Retriever of three years old.

Often, after a hard day's walk, I watch TV programmes about Animals all around the world. And sometimes I doze off. The Animals get into my dreams and it's like a Zoo of Dreams in my head.

One day I made up some Poems about the Animals in my Dream Zoo. I whispered them into my Dogfather's ear. "Those are very good poems, Daisy Dog," he said. He ran upstairs and typed them out for me. And here they all are.

So come for a walk round my Dream Zoo with me and meet my Animals.

Yours with best woofs and wags,

Daisy Dog

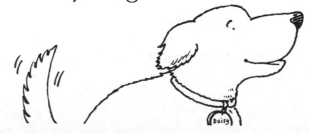

I usually start the Zoo day
by sitting in the bandstand
and singing this song – very loudly!

Good Morning Animals

Wake up, Animals!
Cock-a-doodle do!
Let the dawn chorus
Ring around the Zoo!

Stretch that leg
Spread that wing
Yawn that yawn
Start to sing.

The sooner you sing
The sooner I'll say
Happy Breakfast!
Let's start the day.

For My Pig Friends

I think it's horrible when Sows and Boars
Are forced to spend their lives indoors
In crowded sheds all packed in tight –
No sun, no moon, no day, no night.

I like to see Pigs stroll about
Looking so stately and so stout.
I love to see them snort and sigh
Taking mud baths under open sky.

Sheep and Goats

Goats are bumpy guys
With funny yellow eyes

Sheep are heavy clouds
Who move around in crowds

Lambs are soft little, daft little things
Jumping around like cherubs on springs

The Job of Being a Cow

The Cow's main job upon the farm
    Is to keep extremely calm.
The cud she chews from grassy hummocks
Is changed to milk in her four stomachs.*
    Only a Cow with peace of mind
    Can give milk of the richest kind
    And from her happiest grassiest dream
    Flows the thickest, sweetest cream.

    *Or is it milk turns into grass?
I can't remember – let it pass.

Keeping a Zoo is hard work,
so I try to take some time off for fun!
This is about my personal Swimming Pool.

My Puddle Friend

The Puddle is my favourite place.
In it I see my furry face.

Its water is blue to match the sky
But underneath it's all mud pie.

I roll in the puddle for a muddy squiggle
When I come out, the children giggle.

The Hare

At the edge of the field the Hare appears –
Well, just the top of his two tall ears.
Whatever you say
Seven miles away
The magical Hare; he hears.

No More Hedgehogs

When I do hear a Hedgehog snore
Or see that spikeball swagger round,
I give a grim and grisly growl,
I don my most ferocious frown;
For once I picked a Hedgehog up
And could not put him down.
In my small jaws he was too big –
That pesky, thorny pricklepig.

The Hedgehog Replies

Oh Dog, thou art most ignorant and rude –
Nature did not design me to be chewed.

Tyger Tip

If you go down
To Tyger Town
(Which is famous for gory dramas)
Avoid an attack –
Wear orange and black
Stripey silk pyjamas.

Not all Animals are friendly all the time –
I am certainly not a cowardly Dog –
but I do try to be sensible.

Meeting a Lion

I saw the Sun resting on a sandy hill
The Sun yawned
He stretched forwards
He stretched backwards
On his four golden legs

The Sun sat on the sandy hill
The Sun gazed around him
His yellow eyes
Stared into my brown eyes
And his deep growl shook the earth

I moved away, backwards,
Little by little.
Then suddenly I turned and ran.
Way behind me I thought I heard
The laughter of the Sun.

Most of the Cats in the Dream Zoo live in the Orchard Area.
I'm fond of Cats and especially like to chase them.
I try to understand their Problems, but they are touchy.

Cats

Sometimes they treat me
As their Mummy
Purring and walking
Under my tummy

Sometimes they treat me
As the worst of foes
They spikle up their fur
They scratch my nose

You know where you stand
With a Wasp or a Rat
But you never ever
Know with a Cat

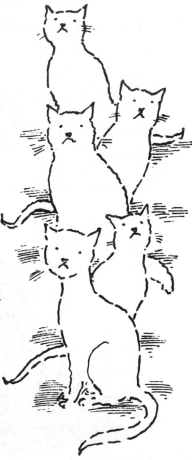

Wolfie

The Wolf's my cousin
But when he howls
He sounds like a dozen
Treacle-covered owls

Dogs wander in and out of my Zoo.
Here's a new friend.

New Pup on the Block

I met this Dog
Cliff is his name
His face and bum
Look much the same

He has a great mop
Of hair at each end
My very furry
Floppy friend

Which way round
Are you standing, Cliff?
If you want to be sure,
Better take a sniff.

My Flower Friends

I love Violets
  dig 'em up

I love Daffodils
  dig 'em up

I love Snowdrops and Tulips and Forget-me-Nots
  dig 'em up

I don't love Roses
Roses can bite you

It's not all Animals in my Dream Zoo.
I like nearly all People
except Shouters and Kickers.

My People Friends

The more I wag my tail
The more they smile
The more they smile
The more I wag my tail

The more I wag my tail
The more they pat me
The more they pat me
The more I wag my tail

People don't have tails
   Poor old People
I love to wag my tail

My Children Friends

Their heads are often muddly –
But they're always cuddly.

When all is still and quiet
or when the animals are taking a nap
are the best times to look out for the rarest
most magical
of all the animals.

To See a Unicorn

This is the way to see a Unicorn:

Close your eyes.
See a sandy path in front of you.
Follow that path over a hill of grass and daisies.

Take a deep breath.

See a clearing in the forest
And a pool like a mirror for the trees.

Take a deep breath.
Be still.

Who walks so gracefully down to the pool
And bends to drink the cool dark water?

It is the Unicorn, the loveliest of animals.
He loves to wander in the forest of your dreams.

See his silver mane and his golden horn.
See his gentle eyes.
Hear the beating of his heart.

Be still.

Open your eyes when you want to open your eyes.

Remember the Unicorn.

Once I was scared of Bats –
because they looked like Mice and flew all wonkily.
Now I know Bats
and I am fond of them

because they look
like Mice
and fly all wonkily.

The Smoky Bat

The Smoky Bat
Is an acrobat –
Watch his aerial somersault.

The Smoky Bat
Looks just like Batman –
But that's not the Smoky Bat's fault.

Marshy

There once was a friendly old Frog
And all he could say was "Gwog gwog!"
    Which means: "Come and romp
    In my beautiful Swamp –
There's plenty of room for a Dog!"

Beware the Swans, who
often
lose their tempers.

Swan Pond

I am very fond
Of watching Swans take off from my
    favourite pond
But, to be candid,
I'd sooner they never landed

I like a Swan
Who's gone.

The Swans Answer Back

Dear Dog, we respond
By racing and chasing you out of our pond
We are the Duke and Duchess of these waters
And we protect our Cygnet sons and daughters

Like this –
HISSSSSSSSSSSSSSSSSSSSSSSSS

This is a very special Hippo poem.
Can you spot the rhyme?
It's a very long rhyme with six bits to it.
I don't like to boast
but
even
William
Shakespeare

never did
  such a long
    rhyme.

Terrific Traffic

The reason Pippa got a bus is
To carry Hippopotamuses.

Seals and Dolphins

How sunny the smile of the Dolphin!
How kindly the face of the Seal!
I've invited them both round together
To share in my midday meal.

I must go. I can hear them arriving
With a flapping and flopping of flippers.
"Kindly sit in this bath while I serve you
Your dinner of seaweed and kippers."

Meanwhile, back on the iceberg,
you may meet a large person
on his way home from fishing...

The Polar Bear

The Polar Bear is creamy-white
Except for his black nose.
Only that hooter can be seen
As he prowls through the endless snows.
I see a black nose in mid-air –
"Good morning, Mr Polar Bear!"

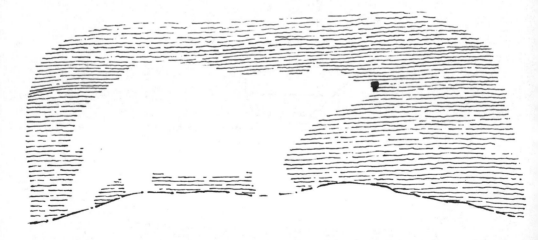

The Little Blue Penguin

All over his beautiful iceberg
The Little Blue Penguin toddles.
He stacks a blue plate with fish for his mate,
Then home to his nest he waddles.

The Little Blue Penguin loves the cold,
He's a chilly little geezer.
So if you invite him round to stay
Make room for him in your freezer.

In my Dream Zoo I don't have cages.
All the Animals can wander where they like –
And that includes the Birds and Insects.

Can you guess who this is?

Riddle

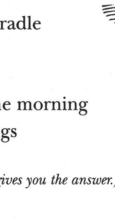

I was a green little
Creepy crawly

I climbed in my sleeping bag
As I felt poorly

I dreamed in my cradle
Of magical things

And woke up in the morning
With beautiful wings

(This next poem gives you the answer.)

Butterfly Ball

Butterflies are flashy dressers,
Butterflies are proper little ravers,
Butterflies wear almost every colour –
I wonder if they come in different flavours?

My Friend The Snail

You say the Snail is slow?
Well, you'd be slow
If you carried your house
Wherever you go.

The Honey Possum

The quiet little Honey Possum
Has a ginormous thirst.
She dips her long tongue in a Banksia blossom,
Drinking nectar till she's about to burst.

Then upside down by her tail she swings
And sings in the honeyest voice I've heard:
"One day I will grow a pair of wings
And become a furry Hummingbird."

Her babies crouch in her silky pouch
Amazed by their honeymama's song.
Then they all join in while the Wombats grin
And the Moon takes a swim in the Billabong.

Gorillas

Moonlight upon the mountains
And the gentle Gorillas awake

They lumber along through the forest
To sit by the side of the lake

And there in the silvery water
They dangle their ticklish toes

And what the Gorillas are thinking
Nobody nobody knows

I suppose all Zoo Keepers have their favourites –
Here's one of mine.

The Glove

An Animal I dearly love
Is an old and woolly holey Glove.

If it's muddy and smelly, it's good to chew –
Especially if it be soggy too.

I'd carry Glove in my mouth all day
But somebody always takes it away.

Humungous

Elephant Millie
Fell in love with Billy Whale –
Their children are great!

Rhino

The Rhinoceros
Looks lovely in the eyes of
Another Rhino.

As the sun begins to set
there is a scurrying through the Zoo
As Animals hurry home to their holes and nests.

Chimps are Champs

Chimpanzee babies travel around
Cheerfully but upside-down
Clinging to the hairy tummies
Of their acrobatic Mummies.

Chimpanzees live in the trees
They swoop through the jungle for miles.
They have good feet for climbing, do chimpanzees,
And very good faces for smiles.

Of course my Zoo has its own seaside.
Without the Beach I don't know how I'd manage at bath-time.

The Pelican

The sunset glows
Like the inside of a peach.
I see a Pelican
Standing on the beach.

The Pelican stands
Looking clumsy and sad.
I want to take him home
To his Mum and Dad.

But he shakes his long beak
And rises to the skies
And graceful as an angel –
Away he flies.

I think I am quite a brave Dog
but just like you
I sometimes get scared.

My Enemy
the Thunderstorm

When there is Thunder
I crawl under
Anybody's bed
And hide my head
And whimper till
Somebody appears
To stroke my muzzle
And hold my ears

Of course we have many fine African Animals.
The Zebra wears an excellent suit
but he's very shy indeed.

Where did Stripey Go?

The stripes of the Zebra
Make you blink
Then he vanishes
Quick as a wink
He's the cleverest everest
Horse I think

When evening begins to fall
on the Zoo of Dreams
the moths begin to
circle around
looking for stars
to perch on.

Jim the Moth

My friend's a Moth.
His name is Jim.
Jim's very bright
But he looks quite dim –
He's not sure why.
When I asked him
He said: "Perhaps it's because a young moth
Has to eat miles and miles of dusty old cloth."

For My Dogfather

I love my Man
My Man loves me
We sing in double bubble
Harmony
When he sings trumpety
I sing gruff
And hold down the bass
With a wuff wuff wuff
Wuff wuff
Wuffety
Wuff.